D0422133

The
RUBAIYAT
of
OMAR KHAYYAM

TRANSLATED BY

Edward FitzGerald

FLEMING H. REVELL COMPANY

Suffolk—and Naishapur

MORE than passing strange is the background of the Rubaiyat. First, there was Omar himself: Omar Khayyam (full name, Ghiyathuddin Abulfath 'Omar Ibn Ibrahim Al-Khayyami), born we know not when but dead by A.D. 1123. Mathematician, astronomer, freethinker, he took the name Khayyam ("the tentmaker") from his father's trade, wrote an authoritative tome on algebra, studied the stars, revised the calendar, and occasionally wrote poems—the greatest of which is his Rubaiyat (four-line quatrains). He was also a fiercely independent, nonconformist who hated bigotry and the narrow mind and who accordingly was in conflict with all pretenders and hypocrites in authority over state and church. Often ill-tempered, blunt to the point of insult, he was the inventor of a clay scarecrow, and his very presence frightened the birds of prey and prejudice.

He loved truth and beauty. He was lazy. When he walked the streets of Baghdad and Naishapur the common Persians said, "Here comes the Master." Others, victims of his barbs, called him a lecherous old drunk and when he was gone went out of their way to spit on his grave. So live, so perish, most eccentrics; *sic semper* the Khayyams. Omar knew that, but he did not care; he said what he had to say and asked only that his grave be a spot where the trees would shed their blossoms over his weary bones, and so it was.

He laid no claim to fame or standing as a poet; he never dreamed that his quatrains would live for long. Now would they, had it not been for Edward Fitz-Gerald, through whom Omar was to become the best-known Persian poet in the West. FitzGerald (1809–1883) was cast in the same mold as Khayyam; he was eccentric, indolent, brusque, a man with a sharp temper and biting wit, intolerant of all intolerance. He loved his parrot, good cheese, Aeschylus and all Greek learning, flowers, music—and books. He was no mean citizen of Woodbridge, Suffolk, where the neighbors thought him important but odd. Children ran from him in the street, but loved him when they grew up; it was whispered that sometimes he walked barefoot in the village street. Oh, well . . . !

He lived there because he inherited a house there, more because he could always "get a glimpse of the sea"—on which he sailed a little boat (clothed in top hat and a lady's boa) in company with one Posh, a poor, illiterate, hard-drinking fisherman who knew well the ways of fish, FitzGerald and the briny deep.

[4]

"Old Fitz" was intimate friend to Thackeray, Tennyson and Carlyle (from whose house he once ran into the street to dance after a hurdy-gurdy) yet he called Posh the greatest man he had ever met. He would sit in church (always near an open window) with a mangy shawl about his shoulders, and he would hum loudly to himself when the sermon became a bore, to the outrage of the faithful and the delight of little boys. Once the parson scolded him for coming so seldom to church; thereafter he came not at all.

FitzGerald never saw Persia, nor Baghdad nor Naishapur, nor any of the East, and was never known as scholar of things Oriental. Yet he took the old quatrains of Omar and did with them what no other translating scholar has ever done: he made them sing a song so lovely that Western hearts danced in reading them. He did not translate Omar; he paraphrased the Persian, so freely and delectably that we scarcely know how much of it is Omar, how much FitzGerald. No publisher would touch it; FitzGerald had to publish it himself, in 1859, in a little anonymous brown-paper-jacketed edition of 250 copies. He gave most of them away; the rest of them quickly found their way into the bargain-boxes of the book stores, begging buyers at two pence—or one. Happily, it was rescued (Rossetti and Swinburne "discovered" it) but Old Fitz was twenty years dead and gone before it became famous literature. He died in his sleep in 1883; some years later a plaque appeared above his grave: "This Rose-Tree, raised in Kew Gardens from seed brought by William Simpson, from the grave of Omar Khayyam at Naishapur, was planted by a few admirers of Edward FitzGerald in the name of the Omar Khayyam Club." It might just be that a member or two of the Club, as a child, had once laughed at him or run from him in the street.

So the so-so-scholarly Briton took the verse of a Persian who never posed as poet, after an interim of seven centuries, and made it a masterpiece. Harold Lamb says it well, in his biography of Khayyam: "Perhaps in brooding over Omar's quatrains, that taciturn Englishman had for a brief moment the gift of knitting cobwebs together, of weighing thistle-down and weaving a magic tapestry of dragon-flies' wings." However factual or romantic that may be, here it is—a thing of beauty and a joy forever. FitzGerald put the Persian in British clothing, and he did more: he created something strangely new and beautiful out of Omar's verse, and made it a gay and lilting moment in the march and singing of mankind.

FRANK S. MEAD

The RUBAIYAT *of* OMAR KHAYYAM

Second Edition

1

Wake! For the Sun behind yon Eastern height
Has chased the Session of the Stars from Night;
   And to the field of Heav'n ascending, strikes
The Sultán's Turret with a Shaft of Light.

2

Before the phantom of False morning died,
Methought a Voice within the Tavern cried,
   "When all the Temple is prepared within,
Why lags the drowsy Worshipper outside?"

3

And, as the Cock crew, those who stood before
The Tavern shouted—"Open then the Door!
   You know how little while we have to stay,
And, once departed, may return no more."

4

Now the New Year reviving old Desires,
The thoughtful Soul to Solitude retires,
   Where the WHITE HAND OF MOSES on the
     Bough
Puts out, and Jesus from the Ground suspires.

5

Iram indeed is gone with all his Rose,
And Jamshýd's Sev'n-ring'd Cup where no one
    knows;
  But still a Ruby gushes from the Vine,
And many a Garden by the Water blows.

6

And David's lips are lockt; but in divine
High-piping Péhlevi, with "Wine! Wine!
    Wine!
  Red Wine!"—the Nightingale cries to the
    Rose
That sallow cheek of hers to incarnadine.

7

Come, fill the Cup, and in the fire of Spring
Your Winter-garment of Repentance fling:
    The Bird of Time has but a little way
To flutter—and the Bird is on the Wing.

8

Whether at Naishápúr or Babylon,
Whether the Cup with sweet or bitter run,
    The Wine of Life keeps oozing drop by drop,
The Leaves of Life keep falling one by one.

9

Morning, a thousand Roses brings, you say;
Yes, but where leaves the Rose of Yesterday?
   And this first Summer month that brings the
     Rose
Shall take Jamshýd and Kaikobád away.

10

Well, let it take them! What have we to do
With Kaikobád the Great, or Kaikhosrú?
   Let Rustum cry "To Battle!" as he likes,
Or Hátim Tai "To supper!"—heed not you.

11

With me along the strip of Herbage strown
That just divides the desert from the sown,
    Where name of Slave and Sultán is forgot—
And Peace to Máhmúd on his golden Throne!

12

Here with a little Bread beneath the Bough,
A Flask of Wine, a Book of Verse—and Thou
    Beside me singing in the Wilderness—
Oh, Wilderness were Paradise enow!

13

Some for the Glories of This World; and some
Sigh for the Prophet's Paradise to come;
   Ah, take the Cash, and let the Promise go,
Nor heed the music of a distant Drum!

14

Were it not Folly, Spider-like to spin
The Thread of present Life away to win—
   What? for ourselves, who know not if we shall
Breathe out the very Breath we now breathe in!

15

Look to the blowing Rose about us—"Lo,
Laughing," she says, "into the world I blow,
    At once the silken tassel of my Purse
Tear, and its Treasure on the Garden throw."

16

For those who husbanded the Golden grain,
And those who flung it to the winds like Rain,
    Alike to no such aureate Earth are turn'd
As, buried once, Men want dug up again.

17

The Worldly Hope men set their Hearts upon
Turns Ashes—or it prospers; and anon,
  Like Snow upon the Desert's dusty Face,
Lighting a little hour or two—was gone.

18

Think, in this batter'd Caravanserai
Whose Portals are alternate Night and Day,
  How Sultán after Sultán with his Pomp
Abode his destin'd Hour, and went his way.

19

They say the Lion and the Lizard keep
The Courts where Jamshýd gloried and drank
   deep:
   And Bahrám, that great Hunter—the Wild
   Ass
Stamps o'er his Head, but cannot break his
   Sleep.

20

'The Palace that to Heav'n his pillars threw,
And Kings the forehead on his threshold
   drew—
   I saw the solitary Ringdove there,
And "Coo, coo, coo," she cried; and "Coo, coo,
   coo."

21

Ah, my Belovéd, fill the Cup that clears
To-day of past Regret and future Fears:
    To-morrow!—Why, To-morrow I may be
Myself with Yesterday's Sev'n thousand Years.

22

For some we loved, the loveliest and the best
That from his Vintage rolling Time has prest,
    Have drunk their Cup a Round or two before,
And one by one crept silently to rest.

23

And we, that now make merry in the Room
They left, and Summer dresses in new bloom,
    Ourselves must we beneath the Couch of
      Earth
Descend—ourselves to make a Couch—for
      whom?

24

I sometimes think that never blows so red
The Rose as where some buried Cæsar bled;
    That every Hyacinth the Garden wears
Dropt in her Lap from some once lovely Head.

25

And this delightful Herb whose living Green
Fledges the River's Lip on which we lean—
 Ah, lean upon it lightly! for who knows
From what once lovely Lip it springs unseen!

26

Ah, make the most of what we yet may spend,
Before we too into the Dust descend;
 Dust into Dust, and under Dust, to lie
Sans Wine, sans Song, sans Singer, and—sans
 End!

27

Alike for those who for TO-DAY prepare,
And those that after some TO-MORROW stare,
   A Muezzín from the Tower of Darkness cries,
"Fools! your Reward is neither Here nor There!"

28

Another Voice, when I am sleeping, cries,
"The Flower should open with the Morning
    skies."
   And a retreating Whisper, as I wake—
"The Flower that once has blown for ever dies."

29

Why, all the Saints and Sages who discuss'd
Of the Two Worlds so learnedly are thrust
   Like foolish Prophets forth; their Words to
     Scorn
Are scatter'd, and their Mouths are stopt with
     Dust.

30

Myself when young did eagerly frequent
Doctor and Saint, and heard great argument
   About it and about: but evermore
Came out by the same door as in I went.

31

With them the seed of Wisdom did I sow,
And with my own hand wrought to make it
    grow;
  And this was all the Harvest that I reap'd—
"I came like Water, and like Wind I go."

32

Into this Universe, and *Why* not knowing,
Not *Whence*, like Water willy-nilly flowing;
  And out of it, as Wind along the Waste,
I know not *Whither*, willy-nilly blowing.

33

What, without asking, hither hurried *Whence?*
And, without asking, *Whither* hurried hence!
 Ah, contrite Heav'n endowed us with the
  Vine
To drug the memory of that insolence!

34

Up from Earth's Centre through the Seventh
  Gate
I rose, and on the Throne of Saturn sate;
 And many Knots unravel'd by the Road;
But not the Master-knot of Human Fate.

35

There was the Door to which I found no Key:
There was the Veil through which I could not
  see:
  Some little talk awhile of ME and THEE
There was—and then no more of THEE and ME.

36

Earth could not answer; nor the Seas that mourn
In flowing Purple, of their Lord forlorn;
  Nor Heaven, with those eternal Signs reveal'd
And hidden by the sleeve of Night and Morn.

37

Then of the THEE IN ME who works behind
The Veil of Universe I cried to find
   A Lamp to guide me through the Darkness,
    and
Something then said—"An Understanding
    blind."

38

Then to the Lip of this poor earthen Urn
I lean'd, the secret Well of Life to learn:
   And Lip to Lip it murmur'd—"While you
    live,
Drink!—for, once dead, you never shall re-
    turn."

39

I think the Vessel, that with fugitive
Articulation answer'd, once did live,
   And drink; and that impassive Lip I kiss'd,
How many Kisses might it take—and give!

40

For I remember stopping by the way
To watch a Potter thumping his wet Clay:
   And with its all-obliterated Tongue
It murmur'd—"Gently, Brother, gently, pray!"

41

For has not such a Story from of Old
Down Man's successive generations roll'd
   Of such a clod of saturated Earth
Cast by the Maker into Human mould?

42

And not a drop that from our Cups we throw
On the parcht herbage, but may steal below
   To quench the fire of Anguish in some Eye
There hidden—far beneath, and long ago.

43

As then the Tulip for her wonted sup
Of Heavenly Vintage lifts her chalice up,
   Do you, twin offspring of the soil, till Heav'n
To Earth invert you like an empty Cup.

44

Do you, within your little hour of Grace,
The waving Cypress in your Arms enlace,
   Before the Mother back into her arms
Fold, and dissolve you in a last embrace.

45

And if the Cup you drink, the Lip you press,
End in what All begins and ends in—Yes;
  Imagine then you *are* what heretofore
You *were*—hereafter you shall not be less.

46

So when at last the Angel of the Drink
Of Darkness finds you by the river-brink,
  And, proffering his Cup, invites your Soul
Forth to your Lips to quaff it—do not shrink.

47

And fear not lest Existence closing *your*
Account, should lose, or know the type no more;
   The Eternal Sákì from that Bowl has pour'd
Millions of Bubbles like us, and will pour.

48

When You and I behind the Veil are past,
Oh, but the long long while the World shall
      last,
   Which of our Coming and Departure heeds
As much as Ocean of a pebble-cast.

49

One Moment in Annihilation's Waste,
One Moment, of the Well of Life to taste—
 The Stars are setting, and the Caravan
Draws to the Dawn of Nothing—Oh make
 haste!

50

Would you that spangle of Existence spend
About THE SECRET—quick about it, Friend!
 A Hair, they say, divides the False and
 True—
And upon what, prithee, does Life depend?

[33]

51

A Hair, they say, divides the False and True;
Yes; and a single Alif were the clue,
    Could you but find it, to the Treasure-house,
And peradventure to THE MASTER too;

52

Whose secret Presence, through Creation's veins
Running, Quicksilver-like eludes your pains:
    Taking all shapes from Máh to Máhi; and
They change and perish all—but He remains;

53

A moment guess'd—then back behind the Fold
Immerst of Darkness round the Drama roll'd
    Which, for the Pastime of Eternity,
He does Himself contrive, enact, behold.

54

But if in vain, down on the stubborn floor
Of Earth, and up to Heav'n's unopening Door,
    You gaze To-day, while You are You—how
    then
To-morrow, You when shall be You no more?

55

Oh, plagued no more with Human or Divine,
To-morrow's tangle to itself resign,
　　And lose your fingers in the tresses of
The Cypress-slender Minister of Wine.

56

Waste not your Hour, nor in the vain pursuit
Of This and That endeavour and dispute;
　　Better be merry with the fruitful Grape
Than sadden after none, or bitter, Fruit.

57

You know, my Friends, how bravely in my
    House
For a new Marriage I did make Carouse;
    Divorced old barren Reason from my Bed,
And took the Daughter of the Vine to Spouse.

58

For "Is" and "Is-not" though with Rule and
    Line
And "Up-and-down" by Logic I define,
    Of all that one should care to fathom, I,
Was never deep in anything but—Wine.

59

Ah, but my Computations, People say,
Have squared the Year to human compass, eh?
  If so, by striking from the Calendar
Unborn To-morrow, and dead Yesterday.

60

And lately, by the Tavern Door agape,
Came shining through the Dusk an Angel
    Shape
  Bearing a Vessel on his Shoulder; and
He bid me taste of it; and 'twas—the Grape!

61

The Grape that can with Logic absolute
The Two-and-Seventy jarring Sects confute:
  The sovereign Alchemist that in a trice
Life's leaden metal into Gold transmute:

62

The mighty Mahmúd, Allah-breathing Lord,
That all the misbelieving and black Horde
  Of Fears and Sorrows that infest the Soul
Scatters before him with his whirlwind Sword.

63

Why, be this Juice the growth of God, who dare
Blaspheme the twisted tendril as a Snare?
 A Blessing, we should use it, should we not?
And if a Curse—why, then, Who set it there?

64

I must abjure the Balm of Life, I must,
Scared by some After-reckoning ta'en on trust,
 Or lured with Hope of some Diviner Drink,
When the frail Cup is crumbled into Dust!

65

If but the Vine and Love-abjuring Band
Are in the Prophet's Paradise to stand,
    Alack, I doubt the Prophet's Paradise
Were empty as the hollow of one's Hand.

66

Oh threats of Hell and Hopes of Paradise!
One thing at least is certain—*This* Life flies;
    One thing is certain and the rest is Lies;
The Flower that once is blown for ever dies.

67

Strange, is it not? that of the myriads who
Before us pass'd the door of Darkness through
   Not one returns to tell us of the Road,
Which to discover we must travel too.

68

The Revelations of Devout and Learn'd
Who rose before us, and as Prophets burn'd,
   Are all but Stories, which, awoke from Sleep
They told their fellows, and to Sleep return'd.

69

Why, if the Soul can fling the Dust aside,
And naked on the Air of Heaven ride,
  Is't not a Shame—is't not a Shame for him
So long in this Clay Suburb to abide!

70

But that is but a Tent wherein may rest
A Sultán to the realm of Death addrest;
  The Sultán rises, and the dark Ferrásh
Strikes, and prepares it for another guest.

71

I sent my Soul through the Invisible,
Some letter of that After-life to spell:
  And after many days my Soul return'd
And said, "Behold, Myself am Heav'n and
    Hell:"

72

Heav'n but the Vision of fulfill'd Desire,
And Hell the Shadow of a Soul on fire,
  Cast on the Darkness into which Ourselves,
So late emerg'd from, shall so soon expire.

73

We are no other than a moving row
Of visionary Shapes that come and go
   Round with this Sun-illumin'd Lantern held
In Midnight by the Master of the Show;

74

Impotent Pieces of the Game He plays
Upon this Chequer-board of Nights and Days;
   Hither and thither moves, and checks, and
     slays;
And one by one back in the Closet lays.

75

The Ball no question makes of Ayes and Noes,
But Right or Left as strikes the Player goes;
    And He that toss'd you down into the Field,
He knows about it all—HE knows—*HE* knows!

76

The Moving Finger writes; and, having writ,
Moves on: nor all your Piety nor Wit
    Shall lure it back to cancel half a Line,
Nor all your Tears wash out a Word of it.

77

For let Philosopher and Doctor preach
Of what they will, and what they will not—each
   Is but one Link in an eternal Chain
That none can slip, nor break, nor over-reach.

78

And that inverted Bowl we call The Sky,
Whereunder crawling coop'd we live and die,
   Lift not your hands to *It* for help—for It
As impotently rolls as you or I.

79

With Earth's first Clay They did the Last Man
   knead,
And there of the Last Harvest sow'd the Seed:
   And the first Morning of Creation wrote
What the Last Dawn of Reckoning shall read.

80

Yesterday *This* Day's Madness did prepare;
To-morrow's Silence, Triumph, or Despair:
   Drink! for you know not whence you came,
     nor why;
Drink! for you know not why you go, nor where.

81

I tell you this—When, started from the Goal,
Over the flaming shoulders of the Foal
    Of Heav'n Parwín and Mushtari they flung
In my predestin'd Plot of Dust and Soul

82

The Vine had struck a fibre: which about
If clings my being—let the Dervish flout;
    Of my Base metal may be filed a Key,
That shall unlock the Door he howls without.

83

And this I know: whether the one True Light
Kindle to Love, or Wrath-consume me quite,
  One Flash of It within the Tavern caught
Better than in the Temple lost outright.

84

What! out of senseless Nothing to provoke
A conscious Something to resent the yoke
  Of unpermitted Pleasure, under pain
Of Everlasting Penalties, if broke!

85

What! from his helpless Creature be repaid
Pure Gold for what he lent us dross-allay'd
   Sue for a Debt we never did contract,
And cannot answer—Oh the sorry trade!

86

Nay, but, for terror of his wrathful Face,
I swear I will not call Injustice Grace;
   Not one Good Fellow of the Tavern but
Would kick so poor a Coward from the place.

87

Oh Thou, who didst with pitfall and with gin
Beset the Road I was to wander in,
    Thou wilt not with Predestin'd Evil round
Enmesh, and then impute my Fall to Sin!

88

Oh Thou, who Man of baser Earth didst make,
And ev'n with Paradise devise the Snake:
    For all the Sin the Face of wretched Man
Is black with—Man's Forgiveness give—and
    take!

      *   *   *   *

89

As under cover of departing Day
Slunk hunger-stricken Ramazán away,
   Once more within the Potter's house alone
I stood, surrounded by the Shapes of Clay.

90

And once again there gather'd a scarce heard
Whisper among them; as it were, the stirr'd
   Ashes of some all but extinguisht Tongue,
Which mine ear kindled into living Word.

91

Said one among them—"Surely not in vain
My substance from the common Earth was ta'en
    That He who subtly wrought me into Shape
Should stamp me back to shapeless Earth
    again?"

92

Another said—"Why, ne'er a peevish Boy
Would break the Cup from which he drank in
    Joy;
    Shall He that of His own free Fancy made
The Vessel, in an after-rage destroy!"

93

None answer'd this; but after silence spake
Some Vessel of a more ungainly Make;
  "They sneer at me for leaning all awry:
What! did the Hand then of the Potter shake?"

94

Thus with the Dead as with the Living, *What?*
And *Why?* so ready, but the *Wherefor* not,
  One on a sudden peevishly exclaim'd,
"Which is the Potter, pray, and which the Pot?"

95

Said one—"Folks of a surly Master tell,
And daub his Visage with the Smoke of Hell;
    They talk of some sharp Trial of us—Pish!
He's a Good Fellow, and 'twill all be well."

96

"Well," said another, "Whoso will, let try,
My Clay with long Oblivion is gone dry:
    But fill me with the old familiar Juice,
Methinks I might recover by and by!"

97

So while the Vessels one by one were speaking,
One spied the little Crescent all were seeking:
    And then they jogg'd each other, "Brother!
    Brother!
Now for the Porter's shoulder-knot a-creaking!"
        *   *   *   *

98

Ah, with the Grape my fading Life provide,
And wash my Body whence the Life has died,
    And lay me, shrouded in the living Leaf,
By some not unfrequented Garden-side.

99

Whither resorting from the vernal Heat
Shall Old Acquaintance Old Acquaintance
    greet,
  Under the Branch that leans above the Wall
To shed his Blossom over head and feet.

100

Then ev'n my buried Ashes such a snare
Of Vintage shall fling up into the Air
  As not a True-believer passing by
But shall be overtaken unaware.

101

Indeed the Idols I have loved so long
Have done my credit in Men's eye much wrong:
  Have drown'd my Glory in a shallow Cup
And sold my Reputation for a Song.

102

Indeed, indeed, Repentance oft before
I swore—but was I sober when I swore?
  And then and then came Spring, and Rose-in-
    hand
My thread-bare Penitence apieces tore.

103

And much as Wine has play'd the Infidel,
And robb'd me of my Robe of Honour—Well,
　I often wonder what the Vintners buy
One half so precious as the ware they sell.

104

Yet Ah, that Spring should vanish with the Rose!
That Youth's sweet-scented manuscript should
　　close!
　The Nightingale that in the branches sang,
Ah whence, and whither flown again, who
　　knows!

105

Would but the Desert of the Fountain yield
One glimpse—if dimly, yet indeed, reveal'd,
   Toward which the fainting Traveller might
     spring,
As springs the trampled herbage of the field!

106

Oh if the World were but to re-create,
That we might catch ere closed the Book of Fate,
   And make The Writer on a fairer leaf
Inscribe our names, or quite obliterate!

107

Better, oh better, cancel from the Scroll
Of Universe one luckless Human Soul,
    Than drop by drop enlarge the Flood that
      rolls
Hoarser with Anguish as the Ages roll.

108

Ah Love! could you and I with Fate conspire
To grasp this sorry Scheme of Things entire,
    Would not we shatter it to bits—and then
Re-mould it nearer to the Heart's Desire!

109

But see! The rising Moon of Heav'n again
Looks for us, Sweet-heart, through the quivering
    Plane:
  How oft hereafter rising will she look
Among those leaves—for one of us in vain!

110

And when Yourself with silver Foot shall pass
Among the Guests Star-scatter'd on the Grass,
  And in your joyous errand reach the spot
Where I made One—turn down an empty Glass!

TAMÁM